The Kugel Valley
KLEZMER
BAND

written by

Joan Betty Stuchner

illustrated by

Richard Row

Crocodile Books, USA

An imprint of Interlink Publishing Group, Inc.

New York • Northampton

www.interlinkbooks.com

This book is for Tom and Dov, and in memory of my father Myer (Meir Dov) Stuchner, who loved good music and good noodle kugel. With thanks to Tova Snider, Karen Shaw, Sheila Dalton, and Diane Kerner.

—*J.B.S.*

To Annemarie,
with love
—*R.R*

The paintings for this book were created in oil on pre-gessoed canvas.
A wash of raw sienna was used as ground coat,
with layers of colors built upon it from dark to light.

First American edition published 2002 by

Crocodile Books
An imprint of Interlink Publishing Group, Inc.
99 Seventh Avenue, Brooklyn, NY 11215 and
46 Crosby Street, Northampton, MA 01060
www.interlinkbooks.com

Library of Congress Cataloging-in-Publication Data

Stuchner, Joan Betty.
The Kugel Valley Klezmer Band / written by Joan Betty Stuchner;
illustrated by Richard Row.
p. cm.
Summary: Ten-year-old Shira has been watching
Isaac play the fiddle in the Kugel Valley Klezmer Band ever since she
was a baby, so when Isaac gets sick and cannot perform, Shira
surprises everyone by filling in for him.
ISBN 1-56656-430-1
[1. Klezmer music--Fiction. 2.
Jews--Canada--Fiction.
3. Canada--Fiction.]   I. Row, Richard, ill. II. Title.
PZ7.S93756 Ku 2001
[E]--dc21
2001004345

Printed and bound in Korea

The people of Kugel Valley were proud of many things. They were proud of their kugel, of course. People from far and wide loved their kugel, the noodle pudding made from a secret, Old Country recipe. The people of Kugel Valley were also proud of their peaceful village, and the farms that surrounded it.

But more than anything else they were proud
of their klezmer band. A klezmer band — in
case you haven't heard — is a group of traveling
musicians who play at weddings and parties,
dances and bar mitzvahs, and even in the street.
Without klezmers there would be no laughter,
no joy, and worse — no dancing!

The Kugel Valley Klezmer Band consisted of Benny on the bass, Yossi on the clarinet, and Isaac on the fiddle. You couldn't possibly have a klezmer band without a fiddle player, and Isaac was the best.

Now Yossi had a young daughter called Shira, and Shira had a dream — to play fiddle in a klezmer band. And it also happened that Isaac wanted to retire from the klezmer band so he could spend his days fishing and his nights reading.

But Yossi said, "You can't retire, Isaac — who'll take your place? You are the finest fiddle player this side of Nova Scotia!"

"I can play fiddle," piped up Shira. But her papa just smiled.

"Shira, no ten-year-old girl has ever played in a klezmer band. Especially a ten-year-old girl who's never had a music lesson. It is not possible."

Shira disagreed. "Papa, this is Canada, where *anything* is possible."

But Yossi shook his head. "Even in Canada, *some* things are not possible."

So Isaac did not retire, and the only thing Yossi let his daughter do was pass the hat after each of the Kugel Valley Klezmer Band's performances.

But Shira wouldn't give up her dream. From the time she was a baby, she had been carefully watching Isaac play the fiddle. Oh, yes, she tapped her toes to the sound of Papa's clarinet and snapped her fingers with Benny's bass. But it was the fiddle she loved best.

Now Isaac noticed how Yossi's daughter watched him. So he found some odd pieces of wood, took a few of his old strings, and made her a toy fiddle and bow.

Shira was overjoyed!

Isaac told her, "When I was your age, I too fell in love with the fiddle. So I'll give you the same advice my uncle Zevi gave to me — and *he* was the finest fiddler in Lublin. 'Practice,' Uncle Zevi told me. 'Practice, practice, practice.' "

"Practice," repeated Shira. "Is that how you got to be the finest fiddler this side of Nova Scotia?"

Isaac nodded. "That's how."

So Shira practiced.

Shira hid her patchwork fiddle in the steamer trunk under her bedroom window. Each day after school, when her chores and homework were done, she took it out of its hiding place and into the Kugel Valley forest. There she played and played, all the tunes she'd learned from watching Isaac.

She played for the squirrels and she played for the trees. She played for the sparrows and she played for the bees. And before too long, Shira thought she sounded pretty good. But was she good enough? Good enough to play a *real* fiddle?

One day the Kugel Valley Klezmer Band was invited to play at a wedding. As usual, Shira sat in a corner watching Isaac play his shiny, chestnut-colored fiddle. She mimed his movements and tapped her feet and longed with all of her soul to hold a real fiddle and bow — just once.

After they had played, the band ate and drank with the wedding guests. Everyone made a fuss of Shira. She ate lots of cake and noodle kugel, and then she passed the hat. The Kugel Valley Klezmer Band had been a huge success yet again. The hat overflowed with coins.

The rabbi said to Yossi, Isaac, and Benny, "You must come back to play for our Hanukkah party this year. Now don't forget!"

But when Hanukkah came around, a catastrophe came with it. Isaac fell ill with a bad cold. No amount of chicken soup or even noodle kugel could help. Benny and Yossi and Shira stood in Isaac's kitchen with dismay written all over their faces.

"You'll have to play without him," said Isaac's wife, Goldi, as she applied a poultice to Isaac's head.

Yossi sighed. "Well," he said, "I suppose you're right."

Isaac nodded, but the nod brought on a sneeze and he blew his nose into a big red handkerchief. It was a very unmusical sound.

Wearing glum faces Yossi and Benny wished Isaac a speedy recovery, then set off into the winter's night for the party. But Shira said, "I think I'll keep Isaac company, Papa. I'm not in a party mood."

The truth was that Shira could not imagine the Kugel Valley Klezmer Band without Isaac's wonderful fiddle playing.

Meanwhile, at the village hall, the Hanukkah party was about to begin. The guests were arriving and the room hummed with chatter and laughter as the two remaining members of the klezmer band nervously tuned their instruments.

Suddenly a man in the crowd noticed Yossi and Benny. He pointed and shouted above the festive sounds, "Hey, wait a minute. Where's the fiddle player?"

The chatter and laughter stopped. Everyone turned to look at the stage. For a few tense moments there was absolute silence. You could have heard a noodle drop.

Yossi opened his mouth to apologize and explain, when a voice rang out from the back of the room.

"Wait! Papa! Here I am!"

All heads turned. There at the door stood Shira, clutching Isaac's fiddle and bow. She hurried forward and stepped onto the stage. Yossi began to protest as everyone else stared in amazement. But Shira wasn't scared. Excitement fluttered through her like butterflies.

Shira lifted the fiddle. She lifted the bow. She tapped her right foot. She tapped her left. Then the fiddle took off like a runaway train. Yossi and Benny had no choice but to play along and try to keep up. In no time at all the crowd just couldn't stand still.

Each man, woman, and child was dancing so hard the room itself joined in. The tables danced, the chairs danced and the roof almost danced from the beams. Outside in the street the dogs danced and the cats danced and the tethered horses stamped their hooves.

When the band finally took a break, the crowd plied them with food and congratulations. *"Mazel tov, mazel tov!* Have some latkes, have some *tsimmes*, have some noodle kugel. Such music! Such a fiddle player!"

Shira drank a glass of lemon tea and couldn't wait to get back on the stage for an encore.

At the end of the night the rabbi told Yossi, "Thanks to your band, that was the best Hanukkah party we've ever had." And when Shira went around the room afterwards she needed *two* hats to hold all the coins.

On the way home Shira told Yossi and Benny about the fiddle Isaac had made for her. How she'd watched him play from the time she was a baby, and how she'd been secretly practicing in the forest.

Shira looked up at her papa. "Isaac lent me his fiddle just for tonight. It was his idea. Doesn't it make a beautiful sound, Papa?"

Yossi gave his daughter a hug. "Beautiful," he whispered, "absolutely beautiful."

On the last night of Hanukkah, after Mama had lit all eight candles in the menorah, and the family had eaten lots of latkes and applesauce and noodle kugel, Shira's papa handed her a parcel.

"Your Hanukkah gift, Shira. May it bring you as much joy as you have brought to us." And he put his arm around Mama.

Shira's heart almost stopped. She could see by the shape of the parcel what was inside — even under all the fancy paper and bows of blue ribbon.

Off came the paper. Off came the ribbon. Shira opened the case, and there, inside, lay a shiny new fiddle, the color of honey candy.

"Play for us," said Mama, so Shira did. And Papa and Mama danced and danced as Shira played and played.

And as far as I know, she's playing still.